LET'S TALK THINGS OVER, LORD

LET'S TALK THINGS OVER, LORD

Derek Valentine.

BISHOPSGATE PRESS

© 1989 Derek Valentine

British Library Cataloguing in Publication Data
Valentine, Derek
Let's talk things over, Lord.
1. Young persons. Christian life. Prayers. Devotional
works
I. Title
242′ .83

ISBN 1-85219-090-6

All enquiries and requests relevant to this title should be sent to the
publisher, Bishopsgate Press Ltd., 37 Union Street, London SE1 1SE

Printed by Whitstable Litho Printers Ltd., Millstrood Road,
Whitstable, Kent

CONTENTS

Introduction

Jesus taught his disciples to pray and put much value on the need to do this. We read in the Gospel how he himself withdrew from the rough and tumble of everyday life to pray to His Father and our Father. But He warned His disciples that they should "not go babbling on like the heathen" and he underlined the fact that Our Father knows of our needs before we ask Him.

It seems clear that prayer is an activity we should engage in, although at the same time praying is not an easy activity. I think most of us fall into the trap of babbling on when we pray. This is partly because we are not practised in prayer; praying is something we reserve for special occasions. We ask God *for* things and we judge the worthiness of what we do by the results obtained. In this way, consciously or not we are attempting to manipulate God: certainly we are not praying.

As young children, taught by our parents, and perhaps our godparents too, to "say our prayers", we repeat words and phrases which have no real meaning for us. Then as we progress through adolescence to adult status we find that the saying of prayers by rote becomes artificial and of little worth. True we may still call on God to help in times of trouble - but He then becomes little more than an insurance against the problems of life. Again this is not really praying however sincere we may consider our pleading to be and however real and distressing the situation we want to change.

Jesus taught his disciples to pray. Not to pray for something. Not to pray only when troubles surrounded them. But to pray. This is a continual and continuing activity in which the disciples engaged with God so as to become more aware of Him. To become alive and alert to his will and to receive the grace and strength to carry this out. So we must pray constantly. But how do we pray?

As well as teaching us to pray, Jesus taught us to pray to God our Father. I believe that praying is a specialised way of listening and sharing. Of course we bring our problems, our difficulties, our concerns and our cares to our Heavenly Father. But we do this so as to share them with Him. We do not burden Him with our problems in order to expect a ready-made solution from Him. For praying is about the world and about relationships between men and women and God. The difficult situations which we all encounter each day are not usually capable of solution like a mathematical problem. But there is normally a resolution which through patience, love and endurance we pray that we may be able to bring about with God's help. So we engage with God on a journey of exploration through life's way, and, by listening, we become aware of how we should act for good in and on the world.

In this small book I have set out to stimulate thoughts and ideas about God which I hope will allow people to come nearer to Him in prayer. I have also tried to discuss a number of problem subjects which concern us all and which perhaps are a stumbling block to some who feel they need to pray but find it hard to see God and His love amongst so many tragic things in their lives. I am aware that what I have written barely uncovers the surface of a complex and complicated subject. But I hope all who want to learn to pray will use this small book and find in it encouragement to set out on the adventure of prayer.

God's Glory

The majesty and splendour of God inspire
in me wonder, love and praise.

You are too wonderful for me to understand.
You are too marvellous for me to think about.
All that I look up to - the goodness and the greatness
and the splendour of this world - is your glory.
Yet it is only a part of your glory - most I cannot see: I
cannot feel: I cannot touch: I can only know.
I am caught up in you and your glory and I respond in
love.
What do I love? whom do I love? why do I love?
Above the weakness and the woe of life and living I
look beyond to you. Love is the only response to you
in glory. I know, but I cannot understand. I am only
because you are. I love because with you there is no
alternative. You are the goodness and the greatness.
So I praise and sing and exalt. Thanks be to God - who
was and is and ever shall be.

The Holy Spirit – Our Comforter

God comes to us not with soothing words nor with comfortable promises of security and safety. When we dedicate ourselves to Him we are at risk: we find we are at odds with the world which offers cheap success and worthless values. God's Comforter is the Holy Spirit - the dynamic of His grace and love through which we can help to change the counterfeit world man has created. In this world, burdened and subdued by the manipulation and misuse of power, the revitalising power of God's Holy Spirit drives us forward with such burning intensity until we are exposed to the dangers built into the sham world around us. But this exposure is our strength and assurance that we are not alone and defenceless. Armed with the love of God, clothed in His mercy and grace we share the splendour and majesty of His glory. Wearing the humility of Christ we experience the overwhelming strength of the Spirit of God - the true Comforter.

―――――――――

I know I cannot stay listless and inactive, Lord. I know I share your glory and it is comforting to be your child. I want things to stay that way although I know you want me and need me to work for you. But your Holy Spirit won't leave me alone: I want some peace

Lord, instead of which I am driven on relentlessly until I am intoxicated with the power of your Spirit. Power is dangerous Lord: it hurts: it kills: it maims and disfugures. I would rather not become powerful Lord. Do I have to use this searing searching overwhelming power which you give me?

My child, how can you work for me without using it? asks the Lord. Use is the right word: not misuse. Power has to be used sparingly and with love. Peace is the goal we seek - you and I. Love, peace and joy are the fruits of the Spirit. Let my Spirit take hold of you: let my love overwhelm you: let my joy radiate from you. Then go out and embrace the world. Open your heart: hold out your arms and let the new power within you become that peace which you know is my gift to the world.

The Harvest of God's Spirit

"All things bright and beautiful — all creatures great and small". The radio blares out this hymn sung by a gathering of children at their Harvest Festival Service. Then comes "We plough the fields and scatter — the good seed on the land". Its all so predictable, Lord, noisy singing of platitudinous words thanking you for giving us so much. The air is full of a false emotion which makes me feel rather sick. It's a bit of a sham, and more of a shame when so many people have so little to live on. Of course it is right that we should thank you for our harvest; how quickly we should complain when the harvest fails. But the truth we know is that year by year our harvest is secure. So this kind of organised thanksgiving is a bit shallow and makes me feel rather ashamed because I have so much. I want to help, but what can I do? Lord show me how I can help spread your harvest for the good of all and the improvement of my brothers' standard of life.

My child, you seem to be a little bit desperate and near to despair. That makes you cynical about things, and I would not want you to spoil yourself in that way. I am very glad you look on it as "my harvest" because that shows that you know about me – your God. And it shows that you do respect me as your God. But you have to learn to trust me as well. You find that very hard, don't you? This is because I suspect that like a lot of people you feel that I am in some way to blame for letting people starve and suffer. You feel that I allow troubles and disasters to overtake people and yet seemingly I am indifferent to it all. You think to yourself that you know what you would do if you were God, so why don't I do it? But love does not work like that you know. Love wants the best for everyone and a loving God as I am tries to make sure that this comes about. But you have to understand that the world of land and sea, time and space is only part of my Kingdom. It is the part I have created and given to you and your fellow human beings to inhabit and develop, not without me, but in co-operation with me. You will know sufficient about the world. I am sure, to understand that co-opeartion between human beings, my children, is difficult to achieve. How much harder then it is for you all to co-operate with each other and with me to create the kingdom on earth. So things can and do go wrong with sad and often tragic results in human terms. I don't want that to happen but I am bound by the "co-operation aspect" as you are. If I interfered and ordered change I would be a dictator God and not a God of love.

Of course it is right for you to show and to express your concern for the physical well-being of your brothers and sisters. But if you feel hurt for them, don't despair. Because as well as sharing the earth's good gifts I want you also to strive to bring about better conditions so that the ingathering of the harvest may be spread and shared in a more effective way. I want you to trust me and to come to love me in spite of your doubts and qualms. I want you to help to develop with me, and for the good of all, the harvest of my spirit – love, joy, peace and goodness. I need you to help me build up my kingdom. By all means seek to bring about better conditions so that you and all my children may have the requisite needs to satisfy human wants. But have enough faith and trust to realise that I will provide, and I need you to help me to do this and to bring in the harvest of those fruits of the spirit which will allow all to be gathered into me, their God.

Holy Spirit - The Wind of Change

We are together Lord - You and I. The quiet and the stillness are shattering because now I am aware of my failings and my shortcomings. When I am alone with you I am forced to face myself. I need your help now: how can I become loving and obedient? Change the raw and rough material of me into the perfect child you want me to be.

Here I am Lord.
Nervous, silly and undeserving.
Here I am Lord searching for you: waiting for you.
I need the power and strength of your Holy Spirit to blow away my weakness and my weaknesses: to lift me above myself: to enable me to reach my potential as your child.
Come mighty moving holy wind - refresh my soul, remove my fears and bind me to the stream of God's eternal love. Then let that love flow through me until I overflow with His goodness, love and endless joy.

Jesus Our Friend And Helper

Jesus, the man for others, the friend of
sinners, a friend yet always King of Kings
and Lords of Lords. Through his presence
we are supported and sustained as we
submit ourselves to Him. We approach
Him as a child, in trust, obedience and love.

Jesus, Lord, let me feel
Your presence near as here I kneel
In humble faith and hope and trust
To be like you is all I ask.

Jesus, Lord, I am your child
However lazy, slack and wild
You will never let me stray
Although I wander from your way.

Jesus, Lord, let me hear
Your gentle call to calm my fear,
Keep me always in your care
When I am lost to know you're there.

Jesus, Lord, I want to be
Your loving child obediently
Listening through the noise of life
To your voice that stills the strife.

Jesus, Lord, take me now
And in your strength I make this vow
To live each day in love and peace
And let my loving never cease.

———————————————

A Prayer on Waking

Lord help me to shine as your light today
I would like to shine so brightly that others will notice
you in me
Give me the humility to realise that it is you I show to
the world
And whenever I get in the way so that the light of you
is shielded from others please remind me to move
over.

Lord help me to speak lovingly to others today
I should like to think I am going to be your love in my
part of the world today
And I realise that means I must not become irritated,
cross or impatient.
Help me Lord to be less like me and more like you.

Lord I ask you to help me to be composed and
compassionate whatever is in store for me today.
Let me know that you are there even if it seems my
small world is falling apart.
Give me enough courage always to look to you and to
hang on to you
And always to remember that you and your love are
sufficient for others and for me.

I Need You Lord

Heavenly Father, Lord most high,
Creator of the earth and sky,
Look on me, your child, I pray,
Guide and guard me, Lord, today.

Heavenly Father, Lord of Lords
I wish that I could find the words
To sing your praise along the way
I walk with You, my Lord. today.

Heavenly Father, King of Kings
You are more than all those things
That flatter, please and lead astray
I need your help, Lord, day by day.

The Lord My Hope

You are my last hope, Lord,
Everyone else has let me down.
I am on my own - alone and afraid
So I come to you,
You are my last hope, Lord.

You are my only hope, Lord.
As I try to face things by myself
I feel and know that you are there
So I am not alone - I am no longer afraid.
You are my hope, Lord, and the hope of the whole
world.

I Want To Be A Child Of God

Make me your light, Lord,
Burning and strong;
Make me your child, Lord,
Spurning the wrong.

Make me your voice, Lord,
Singing so clear;
Make me your child, Lord,
Knowing you're here.

Make me your hands, Lord,
Working for you;
Make me your child, Lord,
In all I do.

Make me like you, Lord,
Happy and free;
Make me your child, Lord,
As I want to be.

Thinking Back Over The Day

I am sorry Lord, But I don't think I have done very well today. All my early intentions: my resolutions to try to be better, to try to be different for your sake, were not strong enough. Its odd how quickly they all evaporate when I am put on the spot. I suppose I haven't enough faith or courage to keep up the effort. I am like seed which fell on the rocky ground - perhaps I flatter to deceive. I am sad about all this because I know I should be different - I can be different and I want to be different. Really I suppose it was just a bad day and luckily there aren't many of them, so I hope I can start again tomorrow. But please, please help me to become just that little bit stronger each day so that I don't just fade away too soon. Let me realise that failing is human: let me accept that now and again I *shall* fail and help me to understand that the difference between what I am and what you want me to become is not impossible. And give me enough courage to understand that when it all seems to be impossible I must not just give up and drift away helplessly.

Lord help me to put my faults behind me and to remember always that you are my one success. *The* success in fact, and let me know that you and I together can win through come what may. I do know this really but its just ...... there I go again. But I am sorry I let you down Lord and I will try my best to see that it doesn't happen again. What a comfort it is to know you won't let me down - I can go to sleep happily now and rest contentedly in your peace.

Lord Its Good To Know You're There

We thank you, Lord, for all your care,
For the food we have, and the love we share.
Thank you Lord, for being there.

We thank you, Lord for bodies strong,
And hearts to praise in word and song.
Help us, Lord, when we do wrong.

Yes, Thank you, Lord, for being there;
Make us all the more to share,
And then to show how much we care.

Learning To Love My Neighbour

It's alright for you, Lord, to tell me I have to love my neighbour. But you don't have to live next door, and to put up with the nuisance he causes. Sometimes its pandemonium around here with his radio blaring, his kids screaming and the constant yelling between him and his wife, if it is his wife. And that is not the end of it, because there are hundreds like him all over the place - So I get steamed up when you remind me I have to love my neighbour, and to love him as myself. If you want me to do that, and to love all other unlovable people in the world, then why don't you change them? It shouldn't be too difficult, but it is too difficult for me to love them as they are. So I reckon its up to you, Lord. Fair's fair after all - you do your bit and I will do mine. At present you put me in a no win situation.

So you think I am to blame. If I hadn't created a world and put people in it then there wouldn't be all this bother, would there? But I did create the world and I have given people a share in continuing that creation. But I also allow them to choose to help me to do this, and to love me and my creation or not to do so. I cannot make people love me and each other. You must see that, because you tell me you don't love your neighbour and ideally I would like you to have more charitable feelings about him than you have. So in that sense I have failed, but only in the sense that the best doesn't happen between you and your neighbours and all the other hundreds and thousands of people on earth. But this is not a permanent failure. The goodness of my love, the benefits of my kingdom, will come for all to share eventually, be sure of that. But your negative attitude will only hinder the progress towards perfection and peace.

You see, what you are objecting to really is the fact that people do things that you don't like. Then you get annoyed and frustrated and you begin to feel that the gospel of love is impossible. Just so perhaps in human terms, but you know that the wonder of my creation, the end to which you and I look forward, is the making of the impossible possible. It doesn't happen because you want it to happen, or even because it is my will that it should. Wicked men and weak men can, and do, thwart my purpose. So before the real kingdom can come you all have to overcome. Overcome your weaknesses, your prejudices, your selfishness, your arrogance and pride. And that means, amongst other things, you have to accept your neighbour for who he is and for what he is. And you have to accept that however unacceptable to you he may seem to be, he is also my child. I have no favourite - all my children are precious to me. That doesn't mean, of course, that I approve of what some of them do sometimes, but nonetheless I still love them.

I want you to try to look at your neighbour and your neighbours through my eyes. Seek for your neighbour that goodness and that love which you know will change him and *make him act as my child in the world. Oh, I know it hurts, but Christ's cross has to be carried and if you don't bear your share of the loving hurt the world produces then you are delaying the day when all the hurt and pain and suffering will be overcome. So try to do what I know is within you to do - love your neighbour as yourself. Don't make yourself so unbearable to him that when his eyes are opened to my love he finds you are not as lovable as you want him to be. Love hurts, my child, but more importantly it heals and transforms.*

I will try more, Lord. I will try to love all my neighbours because you love them and you me want to show them your love. But it wont be easy and I shall need you to help. So don't go away will you.

Learning How To Love And To Share

Lord, you tell me to go out into the world and to be your love. Isn't that rather a tall order? I am not ambitious in that way, so aren't you exaggerating my importance? I can try to behave and to live a good life and I will. But loving and being your love are for special people and I am not one of those.

Everyone is special to me my child. Everyone is my child whom I know and whom I care for deeply. Not everyone responds to that knowing and that caring. You can though, and your response is special to me because it is the response of a loving child. But don't lock up that love and reserve it for me alone. It is my gift for you to share. And that is what I mean you to do when I ask you to be my love in the world. Share the love I give you. Create within you, around you a haven of peace and love. Be my love.

You make it sound easy and worthwhile, Lord.

Yes, it is worthwhile, says the Lord. for love heals: love creates: love gives cheerfully and handsomely. Love is not cross nor put out: never sulky, bad-tempered, lazy or unfriendly. Love is always generous because it is everything that is good shared by you and me in the world, my child. So yes, love is worthwhile. But I cannot pretend to you that it is easy to love. For you will find you will be rejected because you love: you will be ignored by your friends: they will tease and taunt you: they may even hate and despise you. You will become isolated and alone because that is how the opponents of love treat love and those who are loving. In the end your friends and neighbours will give you up as lost and so you will be: lost in me. To love is the hardest thing in the world, but if you fail to love you will be letting the world down. I know the world may let you down, but love never lets anyone down. So be my love.

Lord, I want to love: to show I love you by loving the world for your sake.

Help me to be your love: your peace: your joyful child giving myself so completely to others that I lead my life for you and for them.

Help - I Can't Go On

There are many times when I want to give up Lord. I look around me and see more unhappiness, misery and despair than I can cope with. If I pick up a newspaper, turn on the radio, or look at television I come to one conclusion - the world is just one big disaster area. I begin to cry "Stop - go back and start again". I see the hungry faces, the tortured bodies: I hear harsh words and cries of pain and anguish. I start to cry again and in my frustration I shake my fist at the world - and then at you. "Go on to the end" you say, "Take up your cross". Well I have Lord, and it hurts. I begin to feel I cannot endure: almost I don't want to. You are driving me to distraction, Lord - so help me please.

I think you are little bit too worked up my child. I know there are hard things in life, but the way to cope is to try to understand so that you can deal with them. You seem to me to be trying to opt out. No, I am not being hard or harsh to you, and I am aware that you feel and care deeply about what you see around you. The trouble is that you are looking only at part of my world. You are concentrating on the sadness and the suffering, and you are conveniently disregarding those parts of life which are good and lovely. Don't you get a thrill at seeing a new born baby for the first time? Don't you stand back in wonder at the miracle of that? And doesn't the bursting forth of spring in all its colour and splendour excite and cheer your spirit? What about all the kindness and love that you receive from your family and friends? Do you still think that the world is a disaster area? Of course not. You are disturbed by the apparent paradox of it all. Good and bad exist side by side, both apparently being dispensed in an arbitrary and unfair way. Who is the dispenser though? Now you are in a dilemma aren't you? Whilst you will only too readily tell the world that God is good and wants only good for us all, you find it difficult to believe that the bad and the indifferent come from the same God. But the difficulty with evil is that even I as God have to allow it to happen if I am to retain any dignity as the God you know me to be. Evil, and its consequences are rather like the story of the sorcerer's apprentice. A bad thought engenders others which lead to a wicked deed, and the whole cycle then gets out of hand. I could of course stop things there and then - but if I were to interfere in stopping what you call bad how exactly should I do this? Where would it all end and would I not then be falling into the trap of failing to be a God of love and becoming a despot whom everyone would hate?

No, I believe if you think about these things, my child, you will see that most of life's "wickedness" begins in men's hearts. You and I are here to change that. To overcome, not to opt out. To bring love where it doesn't exist. To show to everyone that the good and the God are for everyone. And to endure to the end even in the face of apparent defeat. Don't "give up" my child, but look up and there you will see the crucified Christ embracing the whole world with a love that is all conquering and transforming.

Yes I will try to do that, Lord. To bear my cross with humility and forebearance - and then to endure. I know it will be hard but my endurance may perhaps help others to see you. And if that happens how humble I shall feel then. But support me Lord - because I know I have to endure for others as well as for myself.

Growing Up To Face The World

I feel sad and cross about things tonight. Work is a bore and nothing exciting happens at home. Mum and Dad just don't understand, and I hate my brothers and sisters. So I have escaped, here to my room where I can be me. But I feel uneasy because deep down there is a nagging in me: a nagging at me. There is no peace - if only other people would see things my way for a change. I know how I want to run my life: how I want to live my life. At least I think I do. Its all a bit of a mess - and what can I do about it anyway?

You can tell me about it, my child. You mustn't despair: growing up is hard and difficult to cope with at times. The world seems to be out of step: nothing goes right. It is not how you would run things is it? But think a moment - are you really being honest and fair? Do you really believe everybody is setting out to provoke or to annoy you? That cannot be so, can it? Think again - hard this time. Could your boredom and misery perhaps be your own fault? Your parents have a tough job bringing you up with the family. It isn't all honey for them either. Your teachers might appear to be dull and uninspiring, but their job is to guide and to teach you. You have to co-operate: to adjust to the things you don't like so that you can enjoy those things that are pleasant. As your body grows and your physical needs change you learn to cope with whatever adjustments are necessary. You can see what has to be done and you do it. But you need to train your mind and your thoughts too. Try to learn to train them so that you can think about others and their needs as well as your own. Try to stand where others are and look at yourself with their eyes. You may be surprised by what you see. And don't think you are clever to rebel - you are just being silly. Remember how Jesus lived the life of a child in an earthly family. He had to learn to be obedient, and to trust those who were in charge of Him.

Lord, I know you are right, but how can I cope when everything seems to be so hard and so hopeless? At times I want to give up.

Of course you do: but don't. Instead look up and try to lift your heart and soul to me -your Lord. I will never give you up and you can be sure that with my strength you can survive and overcome. Be a child of hope, my child; be a child of joy; then together we can bring everyone into the fold and into our Christian family.

Teach me to do that always, Lord.

My child, you know what to do. Go out and be my love in and to the world. You are not too young to do it. But don't shut out the world and don't shut yourself away from it. Hold out your arms to the whole world and you will find me there too.

Lord, I Don't Understand

I realise how little I understand Lord. I accept that your ways are mysterious. But if you want me to work for you in your world you have to help me to follow you. How can I explain you and your ways to others if I am bemused and bewildered? I will always do my best to love my neighbour as myself, to give and not to count the cost, to obey you and to live as your child helping to create your kingdom, to use my talents in your service, and, yes, to stretch myself to the full so that I can bring others to see you and learn about you and then to become disciples themselves. I can even see myself urging others to develop their talents to the full: perhaps even persuading them that they have hidden reserves which, if encouraged, they can put to good use in your name. But when I see a talented person, say a tip top musician, suddenly struck down at the height of his power, then I am puzzled to say the least. Surely making music, interpreting the creative ideas of great composers for the benefit of others, is a service of dedication and love. And yet this ability, this genius, this gift is, suddenly, inexplicably taken away. It seems almost as if you are being perverse. And such a waste....

Well now, my child, I can see your problem, but I am not sure I can help you to understand in a way that will satisfy you sufficiently. Am I right in thinking that you put the blame on me? And do I detect, however faintly, the suggestion that those with a special talent should be exempted from life's vicissitudes whilst the less talented need not be protected? Surely you don't really mean that? You see, my child, I made the world and I love all my children. I love them, not for what they do, not for who they are, but simply that they are. And it follows, doesn't it, that I love the poor and the afflicted: the strong and the weak: the clever and the dull: the talented and those without great talent. I love those who work hard and those who don't. I love my creation and I want all my children to enjoy to the full the goodness which we can create together. But it isn't possible for me to be selective - even the length of your earthly life is not pre-determined. And inbuilt into the world we share, as well as the potential for all the good and lovely things we enjoy, is the possibility of the not so good and the downright awful and wicked. It cannot be otherwise if I am to remain a God of love and you are to have that special freedom which allows you to act according to your own will. If you have the choice you also have the freedom to use or not to use that choice. Now the natural world is not perfect - it has been given to man to make perfect and for him to bring under control. First it is necessary for man to learn in obedience how to control himself and then it is for him to harness the natural forces for the good of all. He is required to do all of this intelligently and under obedience so that what I will, he wills too, and that harmony of perfection which you seem to feel is necessary is brought about. And I can promise you that if you seek first the kingdom of God it will come.

But on the journey to the kingdom there are dangers and troubles and these can and do strike at all sorts of people. That is not something I as your God bring about. Nor is it a state of affairs I want to see. But with your limited vision of my world and my kingdom you see it only as a waste and a disaster. But is it? May it not be that the specially talented person has a brilliance that can shine only for a short period? Of course that doesn't explain why they are struck down, but it isn't a kind of punishment. It is a hazard to which all my children are prone. The important thing to remember is that each and everyone of you should try to use your talents to the full. In that way you will be seeking and building the kingdom. I need all kinds of workers to join in this work with me and no-one and nothing is wasted if you can all combine to give of your best. Whilst having a talent is a precious gift, life itself is an even more precious gift. The development and use of a talent illuminates the way to the kingdom, but my children living together in love and joy and peace is the very stuff and heart of the kingdom itself. So do not despair when you see a talent used up or perhaps stopped in full flow. For the life which nurtured that talent is a permanent witness to the good things that this life of ours is about. Rather be grateful that your pathway to the kingdom has been touched by the eternal in the expression of this special talent.

And remember you are all my children, that I love you all and I want you all in your own unique way to reflect me and my goodness in and on the world. You all have a special talent for something: it may not be a flamboyant talent, perhaps an ordinary one, but it is just as necessary for the building of my kingdom as something you regard as remarkable. It is life, creation and the living together in love which is the remarkable thing in this world and you must all do your best to achieve the loveliest possible life and world for all my children.

I see, Lord, and I begin to understand. Life is not just being a special kind of super person; it is living for you and for each other in your love which makes life special. And I have to use the talent you have given me for glory and not for my own gain. I'll try to remember that I mean as much to you as the world's most tremendous genius, and to be grateful for being able to share some of that genius I have seen in others while it lasted. It is, I suppose, the quality of life lived for you that is important - but it is not easy to understand this without your help and guidance. So help me to understand please.

Frustration

So O.K. Lord, where do we go now? I am just about all in and I can't take much more. I have tried all this business of loving - being a good neighbour, turning the other cheek and so on and what's the result? I am a wreck. People think I am a soft touch: easy meat. I am bullied and ragged: teased and nagged and now I give up. It's the tough guy who makes good in this world and ends up being a hero. I'm just a nobody: a has been - almost good for nothing. So what's the score now, Lord? Tell me, what do I do just so that I can keep my head above water and retain some self respect? I've tried it your way and let me tell you something - it doesn't work. I'm fed up with being frustrated and humiliated so its over to you now.

Phew! You're a bit steamed up aren't you my child? Just keep a cool head and take it easy. All my saints feel like you do. No, I am not flattering you by calling you a saint, just showing you there is another side of things. I know you don't get any medals for doing good or for being good and for trying to create goodness. But who wants a medal anyway? You have to learn to die to this world: to give it up for my sake, to carry your cross in the world. You need to get your priorities and values right. If you want men to praise you then go ahead and be a tough guy:

they will probably cheer you and flatter you but not for long and it won't make you feel any better either. For it is my world you live in, as my child, and you and I have to stand up for those things, those values that we know are reallly worthwhile. Such things as goodness, virtue, compassion and love - those fruits of my Spirit which we share when we live our lives together for others. The tough guy may "make good" as you say but it is not a lasting or an everlasting goodness for the benefit of mankind. Not everyone understands such things as you have discovered but if you give up and give way you won't be proud of yourself you won't get your coveted medal either. Frustration is difficult to cope with, I know, but just go on living and loving my child. Leave me to decide whether or not it works. It does, you know, for it made you my saint - Saint Nobody perhaps you will say, but what's in a name, my child?

Boredom

Lord, I'm bored. I'm fed up. Life holds nothing special for me. I am just a nobody: an also ran. Day after day its the same old boring routine. Get up, go to school, do my homework, go to bed. What fun I get is by trying to be different and daring my parents and my teachers to do something about it. Yes, Lord, I'm bored. And from what I can gather its not much different when you are an adult. You struggle to make ends meet so that when you draw your pension you can get bored more easily. You didn't want things to be like this, I am sure, Lord: life should be lived and enjoyed. But it is boring all the same.

If you are determined to be pessimistic about things, my child, then I am not surprised that you are bored. I should be too in your frame of mind. You are right when you say life should be lived and enjoyed. So when are you going to start to live? Things don't just happen to you, you know. You have to make your life interesting: to use all your talents (and you have some, you know), to change what is dull and ordinary into what can be exciting and extraordinary. Surely you can see that being alive in the world I have given you and all my children is a challenge. This gives you all a choice - either to be passive, dull and dreary people, or to become vital, alive and dynamic. Creation is never dull and boring. Creation allows you to build and shape the world so that my kingdom can grow and my love can embrace everyone. I cannot build that kind of new world without your help, but I can promise that it is most certainly not boring. Perhaps if you are honest it is you who are dull and boring - just a dreary old nobody. So come on then: jump to it and let us see what we can make of this beautiful world together.

Make up your mind that you are going to create something new and exciting each day. It can be done with determination and effort. Then you can let people see that God is not boring. I may be difficult to live with. I may upset your nice little cosy boring life, but I promise you the joy and the love that we create together is the most exciting and wonderful experience in the world. Don't prevent my love from working in the world by being a bore - give yourself to me and see how differently everything and everyone looks then.

Failure

Exams again. I didn't do very well last time, and I spent another year doing the same thing again. What if I fail again? It was bad enough staying down, but I can't face it a second time.

They've just promoted some smart aleck straight from university as section leader over me. All this talk of keep at it Joe: keep your nose clean and we will see what we can do for you: it won't be long now before you get your promotion. All that was to keep me sweet. Good Old Joe, he won't let the side down: solid and reliable Joe. But solid and reliable Joe is a failure in the eyes of the world of his friends and mates. A nice bloke but.....

I'm 39 now and already I have had 2 miscarriages. The doctors tell me it would be better not to try for another child. We can't adopt as we are too old. I am desparate for a child and so is Len. I've failed as a woman, and I have failed him too.

My child, growing up and learning to cope is difficult. In fact it is more than difficult, often it is painful too. When you are feeling the pain, when you are facing a set back you think that it is only you who feels like this. 'They' all managed. Those chaps in the 6th form now just seem to "know it all". It's not fair. He sails through on the fast train, everything falling in place for him at the proper time. And look, there he is - at the top - the boss now. She has babies at the drop of a hat - or almost. Where do we - the failures - fit in? It looks as though we don't. Well now my child you need a bit of cheering up and propping up don't you? I know how burdensome is the fear of not making the grade. I know how the solid plodder is the back bone of any organisation: but he hasn't failed, he has just not been rewarded in the same way as some of the others. I know too how boring and desparate the longing for a child must be. What though are the standards by which you can call yourselves failures? They are society's standards aren't they? You aim for the best: you try to get to the top: you seek what you see as the natural development and fulfillment of your life. But things don't work out that way: you come to what you see as a dead end. And so you describe yourself as a failure. Nobody else sees it that way. I am not denying that you have fallen below the high standard you set yourself, but you are not a failure, - not in my eyes. You, my young friend, can always take another course, find where your talents lie and develop them. Your wife, Joe, still cares for you, and you have a happy home. And even without a child your husband still loves and cherishes you I am sure. In my world I need all kinds, all sorts of people. I need the so-called failures just as much as I need the successful high fliers, because your worth to me as a person, as my child, is just the same whether you make the grade or you don't. Of course, I want you to try to do your best, because that is how you will learn to bring out what is best in you. But above all I want you to remember that living for me and for others is what matters in the world. There are no real failures in my world, my child, only those who fail to adjust to themselves, to their neighbours and to me. So learn how to put your disappointments behind you and then you can be sure you will never disappoint others or me.

Yes, Lord, I see that with your help I cannot fail. Thank you for letting me see my worth to you, and help me to be worthy of your trust.

Suffering

I saw a handicapped child this morning. She could not have been more than 2 or 3 years old. Unable to walk, incapable of proper speech, she was utterly dependent on her mother and others. And I thought Why? Why is this little girl suffering? I could hardly bear it - so much so that I felt I didn't want to look at her. Yet when I did I was transformed by her radiant smile, so warm and warming that I forgot her disability. In that brief instant I realised that she gave something to me and I wanted to hug her for that. Even so Lord, I still ask Why? Why does she suffer?

I cannot answer that as a straight question, my child, says the Lord. But stop a moment and think. Are you not suffering too? Not in the way she suffers, but are you not sharing a suffering which is for all mankind - and for me too?
Suffering is built into the world: whether it is physical pain or mental stress: whether it is caused by the destruction of war or the antagonism of humanity. The pain of being together, of learning to grow and live and to overcome together is part of the way - the Way of the Cross.

Perhaps I shouldn't ask Why? Lord. Perhaps the better question is How? How can I help to let others see that you are there in the suffering? How can I show the smiling face of love, like the smile on that little girl's face, to all the world, all the time?

How, Lord How?

There is only one answer, my child. Look at the Cross of Christ. What do you see? Only love, and love in action. as you look at the Cross you begin to see that the pain is gone: the suffering has been changed. The outstretched arms are the hug Christ gives to all who try to bear God's love. He isn't suffering now. He is giving -giving His all for you and for everyone. That is How my child, and in that How there is no room for Why.

Loneliness

All is still and dark. In the darkness I can hear the stillness: the stillness makes me feel the darkness. I am not afraid even when the sombre darkness envelopes me as though I am being squeezed and pressed between the jaws of a huge vice. No I am not afraid - just alone and lonely. Yes, I have a number of friends and we enjoy doing things together — but I am still lonely. There seems nothing real to latch on to. I don't need for anything. I live in a good home with parents who love me in their way, who attend to my needs, give me a good time and who look after me. In spite of all this I am still lonely - on my own. Life is shallow and without depth of meaning.

Its when I feel like this, on the very edge as it were that I recognise "the other" around me. I become aware that I am sharing my loneliness and I wonder who is there and why.

My child, I am glad that you are not afraid, for that means you are not shutting me out. Perhaps you do not know me yet as your Lord and God, but that is who I am. Your loneliness expresses your need to share - your desire to share, but what you do not yet know. Come closer child: shut your eyes and listen. Close you ears and try to see. Now perhaps you can share my view. And what do you see? A myriad of people striving to break the chains and bonds which keep them from me and from each other. Like you they need to share and to love but they cannot because they are afraid. They stay hidden behind the prison-like bars and barricades of loneliness and isolation. You need to realise my child that whilst I, your God, am always here I need you sometimes to come to me. The sort of "coming to" I need is really a going out to share in and with my world the joy of life and the life of joy. Then there is no darkness, no sorrow, no fear or loneliness. Only love and light which you and I create together. Carry my light and love to the world, my child, for that is how the world will come to see me.

Growing Old

I don't think I want to grow old, Lord. When I say that I'm not being ungrateful for the life you have given me. Its just that I see so many old people struggling to stay alive and finding it even more difficult to cope. They find it hard to cope with everyday things of life, to cope with other people and to cope with themselves. When you are old and need help, it seems it is then that you are left to grow old and lonely and die. I'm still young, healthy, active and strong, and I am grateful for that. But then so many of the sad old people I meet must have been like me when they were young. Now their bodies have deteriorated, their activity has declined, and many of them just sit around appearing to vegetate. They have lost all hope, lost their spirit, and are no use to anyone. I don't want to grow old, Lord, I just couldn't bear it.

I can understand, my child, that you don't want to lose your faculties so that you become helpless and hopeless like some of these people you describe. But they are not without hope if they could only realise it, for I am their hope, just as I am your hope. Like you, I am saddened to see them so weak and helpless. But ask yourself this question. If you don't want to become like one of them, when do you suggest I call you in, as it were? And how do you know that you will be weak and helpless in your old age? For all you know, you may remain strong and healthy until you reach 100, and I would hope you might. The physical world is a changing world of new life, growth and decay. This is the pattern. It is not for you to choose either when you enter the world or when and how you leave it. So don't fret about that.

What you can do is to develop an attitude which will allow you to live your life for my glory, and the good and welfare of others. Then you will not grow old in the sense that you deplore. You will still be able to give to others, by your attitude and your love, that extra something which allows others to see me, and perhaps find me. Such an attitude will not, of course, guarantee that you will not decline physically or mentally. But it will ensure that even in senility you will retain that special peace and serenity which is my gift to those who love and serve me. And this peace and serenity you will continue to pass on to others even when you are incapable of those activities you so enjoy at present. So don't despair of growing old and don't lose hope. My love and my peace are always there for you to give to others and to share with them. You may not always be able to act and work as my goodness in the world, but you can always be my love and a light to others, even when you are old.

Time And How To Use It

Dear Lord, I seem never to have enough time for you. I am rushing about all day - trying to catch up. I have to be "on time". I need to be "in time". I am still here when I should be there. If I hurry I can just make it. If I get a move on perhaps I won't be too late after all. My Prayers - oh how can I say them - there isn't time now but if I get time I'll try not to forget. But there's all that homework and projects and heaven knows what. I am sure God will understand. If I get time I wont overlook to say some prayers. If I get time: but I don't. Dear Lord I seem never to have time for you.

Where does time come from? Where does time go to? What have I done with it? Time is just there - it is the eternal dimension in which we live - eternal because God's creation is the whole of space and time -and more. So I have God's time - but little time for God. Or so it would seem. I haven't really got time to go to that disco party tomorrow, but I shall go. When it comes down to it I suppose I always have time if I like what I do or where I am going. Then there isn't always enough time.

So I must learn to use time - to live every moment knowing it will not return. To see each moment as a precious gift which I can use and enjoy. If I plan in this way there is always time because I shall be able to see ahead past those times I don't like very much to the periods of recreation and repose which refresh me. And one of those periods is my prayer time.

Teach me to pray Lord: not just to say my prayers but to pray and to want to pray my prayers. Teach me to pray in word and thought and deed: to use some time each day listening to you. Help me to learn to value my time with you so that I may understand how to value the time and the opportunities you give me.

Thank You Lord

It sounds so ordinary Lord, but I want to say "Thank you". I am not just being grateful for the things I have although I do thank you for them. But I also want to thank you for this lovely world and for letting me experience and enjoy it. I am a little bit worried though, Lord, because I have so much: my health and strength: a good home: a loving family and so many people and things to enjoy. I am not worried because I have all these things so much as that others don't. And sometimes, too, those people who don't have enough seem to spoil things around them. They spoil things for themselves and for us too. And this worries me and I am concerned too for those who find life hard because they can't enjoy what I have. Then I get more worried because I wonder whether I am only thanking you because I am one of the "haves": and to tell you the truth I get scared at times in case I become one of the "have nots". You wont let me down will you Lord? I really do mean thank you for all your goodness and for being you.

I am glad to hear that you are so grateful my child: that is the beginning of humility. I am glad too that you appreciate this world of ours and the good things about it. I am pleased you show concern for all those who cannot enjoy what you have and who suffer and want. But don't be afraid and cling to what you have because you fear I shall take from you to give to others. Your life is for you to live. I gave it to you with my peace and my love and I leave it to you to make what you can of it and to live it to the full. If you try to work with me then together we can help to build up the new kingdom. So you can enjoy what you have freely. I think what worries you is the element of chance which life seems to contain. The ever present "why" nags at you all the time doesn't it? Why has she got cancer and not me? Why has their marriage gone wrong when we are so happy in ours? Why was I born into a western civilised culture with so many advantages when others live in poverty in India or Africa and are left to starve? Why has my best friend's father been made redundant and my dad has a secure job with prospects? Why?

I wish I could give you an answer to those questions that would satisfy you. And I wish it were possible to solve those problems without hurt and sadness. But although I cannot answer your questions directly perhaps we can look at things together. You see I don't feel you are asking yourself the right questions when you look at these situations. And you have a limited vision of "life". Of course the life you and others have on Earth is important and it is important that you live it out together. If I had felt that the world and people and life were not worth creating I would not have created them. Nor would I have sent Jesus, my Son, to live among you. But "living" in the fullest and best sense is a matter of sharing both space and time which are finite and the eternal which is infinite. Life is not an equation - a set of problems to which man has to find a solution - so that if you are fortunate enough to find the answer you are OK and if not you are doomed. That would be living by chance and it is not what our world is about. No, living life to the full is *the active quest for the eternal goodness. It has nothing to do with the number of good works you do though such works are necessary. It is losing yourself in me and giving up yourself in me and giving up yourself to me. Every child of mine has the opportunity at some time to do this whether or not he knows it. Life and living is a creative activity - you and I creating and sustaining good together. So you see the only "why" in the world which is relevant is "why God". Now I expect you feel that you might want to answer that question in a number of ways. Perhaps so, but just reflect for a moment. Could you or anyone you know or have heard about have created this world? Can you make a flower or build goodness and love? Are you able to place the stars in the heavens or bring the seasons under your control? Perhaps you can now see how "life" has more to it than what you are able to touch and see and experience. Do you not feel "the eternal strand" however feebly?*

I expect as you look around you and consider what is happening in the world you probably feel things do not seem to be working together for good. But don't forget you are looking only at the finite world in which, as I have explained, you and all my children are free to live out their lives as they want. You need to consider the everlasting and the eternal and the infinite and to do this you must reflect on me. I want all my children to share this lovely world and to share me. Sharing in this the eternal sense is not having fair shares as in the welfare state. It is everyone's personal experience and enjoyment of me: and believe me, some of the poorest and the most neglected of my children can and do share in that way more perhaps than you do or you know. "How blest are those who are in need". And it is just at the point when the human spirit is at its lowest ebb - when tragedy as you might say strikes - that those who suffer can find me and experience and share the eternal in the "here and now".

So I agree life is not perhaps "fair" in the human sense but then it cannot be that way. Fairness is only rough justice anyway and what you think is fair others may not. However there are inequalities and injustices which came about because of man's selfishness and greed which distort the balance of goodness and loveliness of the world you and I share. These need to be overcome. The "haves" ought to ease the lot of the "have nots": not out of conscience but from concern. You must love your neighbour as yourself. Thank you my child for the way you concern yourself with and for your neighbour. Go out now and live your life to the full - for me and for others. Always have sufficent confidence in me that you may know that whilst some people seem to be neglected and deprived they are my children and I will never let them go. They have my grace and my love to see them through all their troubles: through that is to that state of "oneness" with me which is eternal life.

Yes, Lord, I think I know what you mean but I don't really understand. But thank you again and help me to see through your eyes and to look at things with wisdom. Help me always to try to live my life for your sake and to trust you so much that I can say "Thank you" for whatever happens to me. To know for sure that only good can come about because you are only about the good and goodness. Then let me carry this message to all my brothers and sisters throughout the world. So thank you again Lord and that includes a "Thank you" from all of those who cannot and do not thank you. Thank you for being there and for being You.

Death

The family mourn the death of their mother. She has so dominated and directed their lives that they are left lost and bewildered now. And father, how will he cope?

The telephone call is stunning. I heard there had been an accident, but it can't be - not Jack. He and the children are all I have. They will be shattered when they hear. Life is now a mess of broken pieces. Oh God - help.

He was only 31 - we had just decided to move. The job was going well: his last promotion had made him happy and we were enjoying life for the first time. Able to live more comfortably. When he went for a check up and they said they wanted to keep him in I didn't worry. How could I expect I would never see him again. I know he couldn't have lived a normal life - but I can't go on. Why oh why?

She went peacefully in the end: here I am, an invalid for these last 30 years: dependent on her, my only child. She looked after me so devotedly - would have made a wonderful wife. She gave up everything for me and now I am alone. I suppose I am being selfish but I can't bear it now.

Death is difficult to cope with when it comes. Even though we all know the only certain thing about living is that it doesn't go on for ever, death is usually a shock to those left behind. Somehow we never prepare ourselves for it: we are not ready when it comes. We tend to live each day as though things will not change. Living out our lives together with our families and friends can be trying at times. Even those who are our nearest and dearest get on our nerves: so much so sometimes that we find ourselves keeping out of their way and perhaps longing for the time when we can move away. Nonetheless we are bound to them by life and by love and in our rational moments we cleave to them because we belong. And then suddenly its all over for him or for her or for us. Or so it seems. And in our sorrow and our sadness we ask why? We look back and regret the hard and the harsh words exchanged and we want to go back and put it all right. To make it up and relive the good times all over again.

Life is a journey - a journey of exploration and development. It is a journey through which we can discover the good and the God, and on which we learn about love. We learn to love those to whom we are bound by special ties: we learn to love others and we learn to love God Himself. Love comes from God and He is eternal. For Him there is no beginning and no end. So it is for those who take life's journey. Of course we encounter many stumbling blocks on the way - but the flow of our life continues towards the good - into the God. And so death is not *the* end but *an* end. A reminder that our life's journey is part of that end-less stream of love flowing into and out of God. The part of that journey we recognise as our physical life on this earth changes when our bodies deteriorate and die. But the journey continues. And so our mourning and our questioning, our wondering and our weeping need only be temporary. Such real and human feelings need only last until we recognise and accept the changed situation our lives take on when we encounter death. That change, like all changes, enables us to grow with God in His new creation which is not an end but a beginning. Death gives us the opportunity to enhance the worth of what we had to embrace the challenge of the new and different direction our journey takes on the road to the source of all love - God Himself.

Heaven

I am not really sure about heaven, Lord. It all seems a bit too good to be true. "There's a home for little children above the bright blue sky" as the hymn puts it is all very well but not very practical. And what is the point of this life if we are meant only to prepare for the next world. Are we collecting points down here as in an examination or competition so that a 70% pass gets us into heaven? Do I have a choice about whether I want to go there - if I don't like heaven it will be more like being in hell won't it? So you see Lord I am a bit muddled about all this. Please explain it to me.

Well I don't really think I can explain heaven. For one thing how can I explain anything about the way you think about heaven, for as you say you are a bit muddled. And there again "explain" is not the right word. You might just as well ask me or anyone to explain Kings Cross Station or a piece of cheese. Such things cannot be explained - they are understood only in the terms of their function or use. So I can't explain heaven but I can help you to try to understand the idea of heaven. Look at it this way. All my children, you and your fellow human beings, live in my world on earth. The earth as you know is limited by time and space and other physical forces. It conforms to certain regulated patterns which you all call by the general word "nature". In man's understanding what happens within nature can be explained. There is usually a reason and one that is intelligible to the human mind for what happens and the way it happens. But as you know, I, God, am outside and beyond the earth and the world: I am not bound by the forces of nature. In religious language I transcend all this. Now understandably when you and other people like you start to think about me you are only able to use your human and finite minds. So again, understandably you think in terms of human symbols and examples. It is a human way to see "life" as a kind of equation: as cause and effect. Obey God and "you will go to heaven". Disobey and you will land up in hell. Such pictorial language is too simple and simplistic. And ideas of this sort paint a picture of a rather curious God. So perhaps in order to undersatnd heaven you should first try to understand me better. So I will try to help you.

Try not to think of me as a man or a person but as spirit. The spirit of good and goodness who directs his children through love on their journey through life to find me, their God. If such an idea is hard to grasp it none the less expresses the idea of "the God within" who works with and within his children shaping the pattern and direction of their lives. This he does not by force or coercion but by love. For I am a God of love and peace and joy. I am that spirit which is above and outside the ordinary - the human - which embraces the eternal and extraordinary. And through our direct contact in the "here and now" I bring this spiritual dimension into the lives of my children. You with all your human friends and relatives and others living as you do on earth are engaged on a journey to find me. In the course of this journey I break in - if you will let me - and so even whilst you are living as a human being you have a glimpse of the eternal - that "other" which is me. The spiritual dimension - your soul - awakens as you respond in love to me your God. Your physical body is not eternal so it dies: but part of you *continues the journey which started at your birth. Here however the simile of "life as a journey" breaks down. Because the journey of the soul to the eternal is not your travelling from A to B but a "travelling with": a going along not "from and to" but "with and into". The further you travel "into" the more of me you find until ultimately we are together all the time. Your earthly vision of the good and the God fuse and become the reality you prayed about and prepared for. The God within has become the God "forever with" - the state of perfect unity - heaven itself. Not the end of the journey but the realisation that yours is a journey without end.*

Those who choose another way, those who choose to travel by a different route, end up by losing their way. Without any vision of heaven and the eternal they fade into oblivion and the beyond. There they fail to find me and so cut away from me they live in torment, turmoil and touble. Their life is hell for the trouble and the torment never cease.

Lord I want always to travel with and into you - to follow the way of life which allows me to embrace your goodness and your love. Help me to share your peace so that I can know the haven of you is the heaven I seek through the whole of life's journey.

God's Peace For A Troubled World

Lord, what can I do to help to bring peace to this troubled world? As I listen to the radio or watch television each day seems to pile on the agony of terrorism, ruthlessness and wickedness. We are becoming used to this now, Lord, - it is almost as though we shrug our shoulders at so much personal destruction and tragedy in a helpless and seemingly hopeless way. I am sure this is not the way you want us to live, Lord. In fact, this for some people isn't living - its dying cruelly and un-necessarily. If you are as hurt by it all as much as I am, can't you do something about it? And what can I do to help?

Of course I share your concern and suffering, my child. It is my peace I want for you all, and I strive desperately through the love and concern of people like you to bring joy and harmony to all my children. However bleak and hopeless the situation may seem to be, remember it is only part of the picture. You hear about and read about only the nasty things that happen. That unfortunately is how some people in society make a living - by pandering to the lower human nature in people which feeds on the "not good" and not on the good. But sit back for a moment and put things in perspective and I am sure you will be able to think of just as many lovely things that have happened as nasty things. Goodness is a shy, retiring and gentle quality which embraces most of us, but never forces itself upon us. The brute force of wickedeness shatters not only that which it opposes but much that is good and worthwhile too, and that is

60

the tragedy in human terms. A shattered and tragic world needs mending and healing, and it is only love which can do this and bring my peace to everyone everywhere. And love, real love, by its very nature is not forceful - it cannot force itself on anyone because by doing so it would stop being love. Peace, really true and lasting peace, is not simply the state of not being at war. Such a state however commendable, is nonetheless fraught with tension and anxiety. It does not allow my children to live quietly and contentedly for the good of each other. My peace is the quality of love working in everyone for the good of all and for my glory. It comes to those who strive for nothing more and nothing less than the uplifting of their neighbours to my goodness and my love. It is, in short, love in action. Love your neighbour as yourself and you will find you cannot hurt him or hinder his progress or have anything but loving thoughts for him. When you act in this way you are my peace and others will share it and the joy which you create. Yes, which you create - for the choice is there for you and all my children to make. And I think that answers your question. Be my love, be my peace, be my joy in the world. Don't be put off by the set backs which the evil actions and the wicked ways of some men bring about. Love... love... love... whatever the price you are asked to pay because the rewards of love far exceed that price and creating my peace is worth more than anything else in the world. Be my love, make my peace, spread my joy - that is your vocation, my child. Together we shall win through, so lift up your head and your heart and don't despair. My love will always be strong enough to secure my peace for this troubled world - a peace which may perhaps pass your understanding, but which you can enjoy with all my children as you follow your journey in the life I have given you. I can't promise that you won't suffer on the way, but I can promise that provided you endure, you will see that suffering transformed and transfigured.

Patience To Wait On God

I find it hard to be patient and trusting, Lord. I know that when I was very young I wanted things all at once. I couldn't wait to know what I was going to get for my birthday and for Christmas, I had to know beforehand. One Christmas I remember my mother found me playing with the train set a couple of days before Father Christmas was due to call. So although I have improved a bit about having things, I am not good at waiting for you to show me your ways and your purposes. I want to plan things out with you, and I am impatient with you for not revealing more of what you have in mind for me. Can't you be a little more forthcoming, Lord? It would help to set my mind at rest, I feel sure.

I think you are only sure, my child, because you think it is only nice things that I plan for you. And so I do, but you may not see them that way. Think about what it is you are asking and what my purpose is for you and all my children. I want you all to live your lives to show forth my glory. That means I need you to reflect those qualities of the spirit which build up my kingdom. In creating you, I have given each one of you some abilities and talents which I want you to develop. As well as developing them, I need you all to add to the general body of goodness and love which comes about when you do things for me and for others. In other words, the only plan I have for you is to become a servant of the world: to give all you can in love and time, energy and understanding for the good of others. How you do this - the way it will happen for you - depends not just on any plans I may have, but on how you use the creative vision you will get from me to further this aim. So you need to be patient, tolerant and trusting. You need to realise that your freedom to live your life to the full is not constrained, or restrained but if you keep it under control you will realise that there will come a time which you will recognise as your opportunity to do something worthwhile for me. So you require patience to wait on how I want you to act or to be in the world. This is the patience that builds you up so you are ready to take on whatever is my purpose for you in this world. You will be amazed at how patient you can be if you just trust in me, your God. Wait for me, your Lord, my child. I will come to you and I will not let you down.